Is Stress
YOUR
Silent Killer?

How to deal with stress and achieve
permanent stress relief

Janet Matthews Dip ION

Contents

☙❧

PREFACE

☙❧

My decision to write this short book was prompted by the fact that I suffered a protracted time of chronic stress earlier in my life. Having read many self help books over the years that were based on true stories I felt drawn to share my experience in the hope that it might help and encourage other people to deal with the stressful situations they might be experiencing.

My lifelong interest in health and wellbeing has also been a driving force in finding ways to deal with stress and to look beyond the obvious regarding the cause of illness and degenerative disease. I am a firm believer that stress is a major causal factor in ill health and disease and therefore I am very proactive in finding ways of alleviating and eliminating stress from our lives.

As a qualified nutritionist I am particularly interested in the role of exercise and healthy eating in stress reduction, as well as being a firm believer that personal and spiritual development has an important role to play in the ultimate development of health and wellness.

During the process of writing this book I became aware of my previous need to have a label and definition of who I was and realized that more recently that has changed and I am now on an inner journey to find the real me, the human being that can be indentified without the labels.

To help my readers have a good understanding of the mechanics of stress I will be discussing what stress is and how it manifests in our bodies both biologically and physically; I will also be discussing in detail some of the stress relief strategies you can use to help you to deal more efficiently with your stress. But primarily I will be recounting how stress invaded my life, how I found ways to deal with it and how the whole experience has completely changed my view of who I am.

I hope that you will find the book interesting and helpful. I personally have found the whole process to be very cathartic as well as being a very steep learning curve.

CRBO

"The world we see that seems so insane is the result of a belief system that isn't working.
To perceive the world differently we must be willing to change our belief system,
let the past slip away, expand our sense of now and dissolve the fear in our minds."

William James

CRBO

INTRODUCTION

☙❧

Fifteen years ago I was in the midst of the most stressful period of my life. I was menopausal, I had 3 teenage children and I was head-teacher of a school for children with emotional and behavioral problems. When I look back I can remember days when I used to walk into my office and just stand there totally inert. I didn't know what to do, everything was completely overwhelming. I had so many tasks to complete but I couldn't think straight and so nothing was accomplished. I simply wasn't coping.

When I got home in the evening, instead of relaxing I was getting cross with my kids because they weren't giving me the time I needed to switch off. All in all chronic stress had taken over my life and something significant had to happen to enable me to redress the balance and get my life back in order.

At that time, apart from being acutely aware that I wasn't coping with life, I don't think I really understood what was going on in my body. I knew about the fight or flight response, but didn't really associate that with how I was feeling. I just seemed to vacillate between inertia and annoyance with everybody and everything in my life.

I am told that many women get stressed during the menopause anyway, but I was dealing with stress of running a school for emotional disturbed young people as well as the problems brought about by three rebellious adolescents at home. I had also given up all my hobbies and evening activities as they just seemed like extra stresses to deal with. In hind sight they may well have helped in some way to redress the balance.

What happens in most stress related conditions such as mine is that we fail to recognize what is happening. We think we are coping and the adrenalin drives us on. It is not until we reach crisis point that we are able to see the situation in a different light.

For me the initial realization happened before I collapsed on the job with fatigue. All of my staff had been off over a period of time with a flu virus whilst I held the fort. The half term holiday arrived, I relaxed, and the inevitable happened. I went down with the flu. Not only did I get the flu but my body seemed unable to recover and it refused to allow me to resume my former busy lifestyle. I was left feeling totally lacking in motivation and depressed. I was experiencing adrenal fatigue and as a result my doctor signed me off school for what eventually amounted to 6 months sick leave. The time had come for me to reassess my life and start the slow journey back to optimal health.

It is because of my own experience and my journey of recovery, that I feel drawn to share it with others. Hopefully I will be able to offer some insights into ways in which you might help yourself to deal with your stress, before it becomes a chronic situation that can detrimentally affect your physical and emotional wellbeing.

CHAPTER 1

UNDERSTANDING STRESS

 CB80

As a result of the work carried out by Dr Hans Selye, (a Hungarian endocrinologist who dedicated much of his life to stress research and was considered to be the first to demonstrate biological stress), it is now generally accepted that stress can be sub divided into three stages:

THE ALARM STAGE

- During this stage the body receives an **alarm** in response to a situation where there is perceived danger.
- This could be as severe as a life threatening situation or something as basic as exam nerves.
- Whichever it is the body comes to the rescue by flooding the bloodstream with adrenalin and the individual will have the choice of "fight or flight".

THE RESISTANCE STAGE

- During this stage, due the fact that the ALARM stage didn't adequately deal with the stress, the body is forced to learn to cope with the situation rather than to resolve it.
- This characteristically results in the typical "not coping" scenario.

- It can also be a time when people turn to drink to help alleviate the feelings of stress.

• THE EXHAUSTION STAGE

- During this stage the inevitable happens. The exhaustion that was a factor in the resistance stage becomes a permanent fixture.
- You have reached the point of no return and something drastic has to happen to redress the balance and restore equilibrium.
- It is at this point that physical illness such as heart disease and cancer can invade the body. We will deal with the reasons for this later in the book.

It is important to understand that our stress system is activated as soon as we perceive danger and as a result it releases two hormones, called adrenalin and cortisol, into the blood stream to enable us to deal more effectively with the stressful situation. This results in various physical changes such as sweating, faster heart beat and heightened awareness. This is often referred to as the fight or flight syndrome and dates back to the time when we were cavemen and needed to react quickly to danger. Our lives are very different now and we are constantly assailed by a variety of different types of stress in our very busy lives. Unlike the cavemen, the perceived danger often doesn't go away.

It is not unusual to hear somebody insisting that despite what appears to be a very stressful life style that they don't "feel" stressed. This is because they are not experiencing the sudden rush of adrenalin in preparation for the fight or flight, as they might have done if they were being chased by a big bear. Instead their bodies are regularly pumping out cortisol and adrenalin to help them deal with more low level stressful situations that don't require fight or flight in the same way, but just require them to perhaps focus more clearly or improve their performance or perhaps to deal with the effects of life's daily grind, such as getting stuck in traffic.

This lower level stress often isn't recognized as stress and can go on for years until finally the damage becomes all too obvious. We think we are coping but in fact we are suffering silently until the silence can no longer be maintained.

This is exactly what was happening to me on a daily basis. I was dealing with low level stress day in day out.

This continued for many years until I became acutely aware that I was suffering from adrenal fatigue and could no longer function normally. I was now suffering from chronic stress.

Something had to change.

TESTIMONIAL

"My mother used to suffer from what she called a "nervous tummy", occasional bouts of nausea and diarhoea. It always happened during times of stress or even when her loved ones were going through tough times, she was very sensitive.

Her sister, who was less empathic and didn't have a stressful life, was never ill.

Despite being older, her sister also outlived her by a good number of years."

Colette, retired Office Manager

CHAPTER 2

WHAT WERE THE SIGNS THAT I WAS SUFFERING FROM STRESS?

○ЗЮ

In my own case the signs that I was suffering from stress were as follows.

- Inertia and lack of motivation.
- Inefficiency and inability to complete tasks on time.
- Inconsistency in my work.
- Irrational behavior.
- Physical and mental fatigue.
- Bodily tension.
- Guilt.
- Headaches and migraines on a regular basis.
- Intermittent backache.
- Inability to cope with everyday tasks.

Of course these symptoms became more obvious the further into the stressed state I became.

Other symptoms that are indicators of stress are:-

- Manic behavior, such as constant tidying up or doing repetitive tasks.
- Anger.
- Argumentativeness.
- Non assertive behavior.
- Hostile behavior.

- Insomnia.
- Palpitations.
- Sweating.
- Weight gain.
- Weight loss.
- Hair loss.
- Rashes.
- Acne.
- Muscle spasms.
- Lack of concentration.
- Panic attacks.
- Hyperventilation.
- Depression.
- Loss of motivation.
- Loss of sex drive.

Scary isn't it? I expect most people will recognized at least two or three of those symptoms, in which case stress maybe quite low key in your life at present, however many more of you will recognize maybe a dozen or more and may therefore be well on the road to suffering chronic stress without even realizing it. There may even be symptoms you have suffered that I haven't included on my list.

It may well also be the case that you don't see yourself as suffering from stress. A common retort from people is, "Well that is just life isn't it?"

Of course to a certain extent they are quite right, it is "just life". But in another sense it doesn't have to be like that. We can do things to make our lives less stressful and we can also do things to help alleviate our stress and deal with the symptoms. Ignoring it just isn't an option if you don't want to end up in a worse state of health sometime in the future.

The most important thing to be aware of at this stage is that the symptoms you are experiencing are possibly just the tip of the iceberg.

They are the wakeup call alerting you to a need to make changes and deal with your life in a different way. A counselor once gave me some very wise words of advice that I have passed on to many people over the years:

CX80

**"If you do what you've always done,
you'll get what you always got!"**

CX80

(Apparently an original quote from Henry Ford, so worth taking note!)

Change isn't an option if you want a different outcome.

I remember a prayer I was taught some years ago that seems very pertinent to include here.

THE SERENITY PRAYER

"God grant me the serenity to accept the things I cannot change; the courage to change the things I can; and the wisdom to know the difference."

We need all the wisdom we can muster when we are dealing with stress.

It is a well documented fact that stress is a major contributor to heart disease, and other degenerative diseases, which is one of the reasons that stress is called the ***silent killer***. It ticks away like a time bomb until one day it goes off. But if you heed the ticking you can prevent the explosion.

The choice is yours.

My mother used to warn me about burning the candle at both ends. When it eventually meets in the middle you experience burn out.

In my own situation I knew I was receiving a wake-up call and my survival instincts, which happen to be very strong, kicked in immediately and I started to take control of my life and started to make small changes that eventually made a very big difference.

CHAPTER 3

WHAT ARE THE MAIN CAUSAL FACTORS THAT LEAD TO STRESS?

CR&O

Many years ago I remember reading that divorce, death of a loved one and moving house where three of the main causes of stress and indeed they are extremely stressful situations that may affect the sufferer for many months if not years of their life. However the full list of causal factors that lead to stress is a long one and even if we are lucky enough to avoid some of the most stressful ones, we are unlikely to be able to avoid many of the others during our lifetime.

Some of the causes will be well known to you, but the likelihood is there will be others that will come as a complete surprise.

I will list the causes in no particular order

- Divorce or break up of a relationship, especially if it is acrimonious.
- Death of a loved one , especially a close family member.
- Illness of a loved one.
- Moving house.
- Financial problems.
- Major family issues and domestic problems.
- Work based stress. This could be for many different reasons including, lack of job satisfaction, pressure, goals, targets, bullying, not up to the job etc etc

- Overwork. This can be in the workplace or at school/college/university, when too much is expected with too little time given to complete the task.
- Lack of workplace support.
- Feeling out of control.
- Unemployment.
- Anxiety and fear. This could be due to many different reasons
- Survival stress, your response to a dangerous situation that threatens your life.
- Internal stress, stress caused by unnecessary worry about something you can do nothing about.
- Relationships. Family relationships can be very stressful, but friendships are often under rated for the stress they cause, especially when jealousy and misunderstandings take place.
- Christmas and other major celebrations.
- Hormones/PMT/menopause.
- Lack of forgiveness, resentment, regret.
- Unreasonably high expectations of self.
- Lack of confidence and self worth.
- Psychological factors such as bullying, and abuse of one sort or another.
- Poor work/life balance, no time for relaxation and recharging the batteries
- Change. Most people hate change and having to deal with change can be extremely stressful
- Poor nutrition. Poor eating habits, fast foods, fad diets, sugar, coffee and other stimulants
- Allergies and food intolerances.
- Alcohol -this can be a short term strategy, often used to alleviate stress, but in the long run, as with coffee, it does in fact exacerbate the problem rather than help it.
- Exposure to toxins in the environment, including vaccinations.

This list is by no means exhaustive and I may well have missed a vital one that you feel is your main stressor. But the point of the list is to emphasize that the causes of stress are many and varied. It isn't necessarily one big event like divorce that is the causal factor of stress, but more often than not it is a combination of many of the other causes that can enter our lives on a regular basis.

MAIN CAUSAL FACTORS OF MY OWN STRESS

From my own perspective the factors that featured highly in my stressed state where as follows.

- Work based stress. My work involved dealing with some of the most difficult teenagers in the county.
- Overwork. The previous year we had our first Ofsted (the UK government's school inspection) and the work load necessary to prepare for the inspection in the early days of Ofsted was unprecedented.
- Internal stress. I am someone who stresses over wanting to get things right, make the right decision, leaving no stone unturned. I would constantly go over my day to see if there was anything I could have done differently or better.
- Hormones. I was menopausal and my hormones were all over the place.
- Family life. My kids were teenagers and dealing with their problems at the end of the day, having dealt with stroppy teenagers with emotional and behavioral difficulties all day, was the straw that broke the camel's back.
- Unreasonably high expectations. Mostly these were my own expectations of what I felt I should be able to achieve. I wanted to be the best I could be in all areas of my life and could be quite hard on myself if I didn't match up to my expectations.

- Lack of workplace support. Thankfully I had many very supportive staff but I had a couple of staff members who caused me some difficulty and subsequently anxiety about how to deal with the issues they presented became a major issue. This wasn't helped by the fact that I felt unsupported by those in authority above me.
- Poor work/life balance. I had given up many of my hobbies and my life had become all work and then I collapsed in a heap when I got home. I certainly didn't have time for any fun or therapeutic relaxation!

So as you can see I was suffering from eight of the causal factors listed above. There may well also have been other isolated occasions where I met with everyday stressors. I was also suffering from several allergies/intolerances that were undoubtedly stressing my body as I struggled to digest these foods, but didn't discover that until several years later. When I look back now I find it hard to believe that I actually thought I wasn't stressed, and that I was coping ok.

Our response to a single stressful situation should cause no real problem. The body deals with it in an appropriate manner and more often than not the stress does not cause any lasting damage. It happens and then that particular stress has gone. It is that adrenal rush we get as we go over the top on the big dipper. For a moment our life is in the balance and then the moment has passed. As I mentioned earlier this is called acute stress and is referred to as the ALARM stage, when the body is preparing for fight or flight.

However there are occasions when the stress becomes chronic. If the stress continues and the blood is constantly flooded with adrenalin, then the body is unable to return to a state of homeostasis, and the stress response remains switched on. This is not a healthy situation to be in and the alarm bells should be starting to ring. This is certainly the situation I found myself in when I had been experiencing the stress for some time.

Now would be a good time to have a look at the list of the causal factors to see if you can identify any of the reasons why you might be suffering from stress.

In the next chapter we will explore how stress contributes to ill health in more detail.

TESTIMONIAL

"I was diagnosed with anorexia just after my parents split up. I stayed with Mum and money was really tight. We were facing homelessness. Anorexia was my way of coping, something I could control. Once I learned better coping strategies, like the ones suggested in this book, and started to deliberately do things I enjoyed (that didn't have to cost money), I was able to get over the anorexia. I also beat insomnia, which had been awful."

Anna, dancer

CHAPTER 4

HOW STRESS CONTRIBUTES TO ILL HEALTH

ᏸᎯᏸ

Stress is a normal part of our everyday life. It is something we come across throughout our lives. Our first day at school, an important exam, a job interview, a new relationship, all of these are situations where we are likely to experience a certain degree of stress.

Under normal circumstances we are quite able to deal with these stressful episodes and it is unlikely that they will have a detrimental effect on our health.

However the issue that I am addressing here is that many of us experience more than the average amount of stress in our lives, and when this continues for a protracted amount of time health problems tend to follow.

As I mentioned earlier when the body receives the stress signal the body pumps the hormones adrenalin and cortisol into the blood stream to initiate the fight or flight process. If the stress continues for any length of time the body is in a continual state of stress and the adrenal glands are overworked.

When we suffer from any form of chronic stress this is the most likely scenario and eventually we will suffer from adrenal insufficiency and as a consequence there will not be sufficient adrenalin to return the body to homeostasis (its normal state)

The other hormone – cortisol, also remains high in chronic stress, resulting in problems with glucose regulation. It also interferes with the hormone progesterone which in turn can lead to estrogen dominance, resulting in the following symptoms

- Fluid retention.
- Heavy or irregular periods.
- Fatigue.
- Breast tenderness.
- Weight gain and increase in body fat.
- Mood swings and depression.
- Low thyroid symptoms.
- Increased risk of endometrial and breast cancer.

Adrenal stress causes weakened adrenal glands which in turn can cause hypothyroidism which is characterized by.

- Sensitivity to the cold.
- Constipation.
- Dry skin and brittle nails.
- Poor memory and foggy thinking.

We tend to forget that our bodies are finely tuned engines and although they can deal adequately with temporary blips, the adaptations required in more chronic situations can cause more permanent damage that inevitably has a knock on effect with our overall health and well being.

Apart from these adverse affects on bodily functions, the bottom line is that chronic stress depletes the immune system making us susceptible to illness and disease.

HOW STRESS AFFECTS THE IMMUNE SYSTEM

There is plenty of evidence from various studies available that supports the notion that stress affects the immune system and in so doing it allows, and in some cases encourages, diseases such as cancer, heart disease and HIV/AIDS.

According to an article in the Psychological Bulletin Nov 1990, empirical evidence suggests that chronic stress not only suppresses the immune system but there is also evidence that it may not even adapt over time. This means that if the body is in chronic stress the immune system may be permanently compromised.

As I have already mentioned, stress produces a hormone called cortisol which alerts the body to slow down other bodily functions until the stressful period has passed. When this has happened the body reverts back to homeostasis. In chronic stress this simply doesn't happen leaving the body vulnerable to attacks from bacteria and viruses and other diseases.

It would appear that stress might cause cancer either by weakening the anti -tumor defense mechanism of the immune system or possibly even by encouraging the formation of new blood vessels that feed the tumor. A more recent study by Anil Sood MD and his colleagues at the University of Texas indicates that stress hormones encourage tumors to grow and spread. The research is published in The Journal of Clinical Investigation April 2010.

Psychologist Sheldon Cohen has particular interest in ascertaining exactly how stress affects our health, how it causes a weakened immune system and ultimately contributes to disease. Earlier this year he led a research team at Carnegie Mellon University which found that chronic stress affects the body's ability to regulate the inflammatory response. It is thought that this inflammation could be responsible for the development and progression of many diseases.

Cohen also believes that another factor maybe behavioral. As I indicated earlier, diet, nutrition and exercise are very important factors and Cohen suggests that people who have adopted poor eating habits are less likely to exercise and more likely to smoke and sleep less. All of these factors will contribute towards a person's overall stress and ultimately will contribute to the onset of disease.

It would appear that although a fuller understanding of the way stress affects the immune system requires more research, the empirical evidence mentioned above remains undeniable.

Chapter 5

Proven Strategies for Dealing with Stress

☙❧

How to Deal with Acute Stress

According to Dr Hans Seyle, a pioneering endocrinologist from the 20th century, there are two types of stress:

- **Eustress** –refers to good stress which is the more pleasurable stress.

- **Distress** - refers to the more undesirable forms of stress that have negative implications.

Acute stress, in isolation, can actually be quite beneficial. That rush of adrenalin gives us energy, motivates us to perform and encourages us to "up" our game.

Eustress might include preparation for marriage or for some other celebration or maybe playing in a tennis tournament or running in a competitive race.

Distress might include having a serious argument with a friend or loved one, or getting stuck in traffic and being late for work.

As already stated, in most acute situations the body will deal adequately with the stress and there will be no lasting problems. However when there are too many acute phases and the acute stress becomes chronic stress, some strategies need to be put in place to ensure that the acute stress and its effects are dealt with effectively and not allowed to get out of hand.

In the acute stage it is probably sufficient to ensure that you have some relaxation time, have a regular exercise regime and maybe some pamper time. I would also advise you take stock of dietary habits and ensure you aren't stressing your body with fast foods, sugary foods and drinks that will stimulate the adrenal glands. I will be going into more detail about some of these strategies in a future chapter.

It may also be important at this stage to remember the importance of that little word "no". Generally speaking we like to please and we also like to be needed by others. When we are asked to do things for other people we tend to put them first and ourselves last, because we feel that is the right thing to do. But so many people's stress, my own included, is due to the fact that they take on far too much because they are unable to say no. Being assertive is one of the most important strategies you can employ as well as accepting that there are occasions when it is alright to put your own needs first.

Of course if one of your stressors is regularly being stuck in traffic and being late for work, then you either need to get up earlier or find another way to travel to work!

How to Deal with Chronic Stress

Remember I said earlier that chronic stress should set alarm bells ringing? It is a wake-up call to alert you to the fact that your life is out of balance and probably many things need to change. As change in itself can cause stress this can be a difficult thing to achieve, especially if you don't know what to change. As with the Serenity prayer it is about "*the wisdom to know the difference*".

Change is vitally important, but it is also important to take small steps towards the change.

I have listed several strategies here that maybe worth your consideration. Some will be more appealing than others but all of them are generally thought to have a positive effect on stress. If you have been using strategies already to deal with acute stress than some of them may well be familiar.

The important thing to remember with chronic stress is that it isn't just about strategies; it is also about lifestyle choices. Change happens successfully when awareness leads us to make those changes, the awareness that the way we are currently leading our lives isn't working for us. We need to want to change so much that not changing is no longer an option.

Unfortunately for most of us, the realization of the need to change comes at a time of crisis.

However, whatever your state of mind at this point, it can only benefit you to add some of these strategies to your daily or weekly routine. Maybe you will come to like them. If not you can always try something different until you find something that fits your lifestyle.

- **Relaxation** – Relaxation can be something as simple as reading a good book, going for a walk in the countryside or spending time with friends. It can also be taken a step further and can include simple meditation practice such as sitting in silence or listening to meditative music. Some people regularly practice deep breathing to calm themselves and indeed this increase in oxygen to the lungs does seem to work. This is in part due to the fact that the body receives the signal that all is calm and noradrenalin is released into the bloodstream to counter the adrenalin.

- **Neuro Linguistic Programming (NLP)** – NLP is basically strategies for re-programming the way you think and behave. It might for example help you to be more assertive or to have more confidence in the way you deal with problems and issues.

21

In the first instance it is probably best to engage the help of an NLP practitioner who can guide you towards the strategies that are best suited to your needs.

- **Nutrition and Exercise**– The effect of nutrition in stress is greatly undervalued. Not only can poor nutrition exacerbate your stress but good nutrition can actually help with healing process. For example eating a balanced diet of good quality meat and oily fish, nuts, seeds, fresh fruit and vegetables will give you the nutrients such as protein, vitamins B, C and E, and the minerals magnesium and zinc all of which are needed to help you to deal more effectively with stress. Exercise also has a vital role to play in stress management. Amongst other things it encourages the release of endorphins, hormones that give you a feel good factor.

- **Alternative Therapies** – alternative therapies such as Homeopathy and Bach Flower Remedies have shown to help in certain stressful situations. Massage and reflexology can also be very beneficial as they help your body to relax.

- **Nutritional Supplements** - can also help to redress the balance if there are nutritional deficiencies contributing to the stress condition. For example stress depletes B vitamins that are needed to produce energy, so a B Complex supplement might be a good idea. In chronic stress situations food alone is insufficient to redress the balance and so supplementation may be a short term necessity.

- **Emotional Freedom Technique EFT** – Emotional issues can often be at the core of many stress related conditions. EFT is a strategy that involves tapping the meridians whilst saying positive affirmations. This is an amazing tool that can help to clear any emotional issues or emotional blocks that may be preventing the stressed person from improving. Again it is worth investing in a session with a practitioner to help you to formulate the practice that will work best for you. There are other similar programs available that also help to address underlying emotional problems.

- **Counseling** – Finding a good counselor can be a vital component of any anti stress regime. I know from my own experience that a competent counselor can very quickly help you to get to a deeper level of understanding regarding what is the main cause of your stress. It is then much easier to start to deal with the root cause of your stress. In my case what I thought was my main stressor was actually way down the list.

- **Autogenic Training** - Autogenic Training is a relaxation technique that takes place for 15 minutes, three times a day. A set of visualizations are repeated to induce a state of relaxation. The technique can be used to alleviate many stress-related psychosomatic disorders.

- **Martial arts** – Martial arts include disciplines such as aikido, judo, tai chi, jujitsu, karate, kung fu and taekwondo. The purpose of martial arts is to train what is termed a "warrior spirit". A warrior spirit can develop certain characteristics that in turn will help you to develop strategies for coping with stress. For example a warrior spirit is able to calm fears and build confidence.

- **Qigong** – Qi Gong means to cultivate the body's vital energy. It is a mind / body exercise that relaxes the body and helps it to transform stress into a healthy source of energy

- **Yoga** – Yoga comes from the word yoke which means bringing together. That is in fact exactly what it does; it brings together body mind and spirit. It also brings together physical postures, meditation and controlled breathing, all of which are very beneficial for stress both on a superficial level and also, when practiced on a regular basis, on a deeper more spiritual level.

- **Meditation** – meditation is excellent on many different levels. It quietens the mind, sharpens your focus, and encourages concentration to name but a few of its benefits. I am particularly interested in mindfulness meditation, a practice that should be done every minute of every day. It is a practice of awareness and of being in the present moment at all times. It is one of the single most helpful practices for dealing with chronic stress and one that I have used, as you will see later in the book.

- **Singing** – Singing has many benefits regarding stress relief. It is a very enjoyable relaxing hobby that can engender a feel good factor. If done correctly it is also an excellent exercise in deep breathing. Belonging to a choir can also be a way of switching off from the turmoils of the day.

- **Art** – Like singing, art is a very relaxing pastime. Art therapy can also be helpful in addressing underlying emotional issues.

- **Organization** – Being disorganized can be one of the most stressful situations, especially if your day demands that you get through a hefty list of tasks. If you have an untidy desk or an untidy house it can be more difficult to be efficient and subsequently more difficult to relax.

- **Time management** – Time management goes hand in hand with organization. You need to organize your time in the same way as you organize other aspects of your life. Having a daily time table and list of tasks to be done will inevitably make you more efficient and less likely to be stressed

- **De Cluttering** – De cluttering isn't just about removing the clutter and putting it away, it is about simplifying your life. Get rid of the clutter, not only in your home and your work but also the clutter in your head.

The last three are also strategies that I have chosen to address particularly in the last 12 months.

Many of these strategies warrant a book of their own, but for now I have just mentioned them briefly so that you can research for further information if you feel any of them are of particular interest to you.

TESTIMONIAL

"My fiancé bought this book and I read it, thinking that there wouldn't be anything in it for me because I'd always been quite a laid-back person. I realized why – I had hobbies and habits that let me deal with any stress: playing guitar/singing, being in a sports team, meditation, and a healthy diet. When my fiancé followed the advice in this book and took up some of my hobbies she found she became more laid back too!"

Andrew, Health & Safety Consultant

CHAPTER 6

HINDSIGHT IS A WONDERFUL THING

०७४०

There is a famous quotation by George Bernard Shaw that really resonates with me:

> ०७४०
>
> *"Youth is wasted on the young"*
>
> ०७४०

If only we had known what we know now when we were younger, perhaps we wouldn't have made the same mistakes. In the same way I feel that hindsight is a wonderful thing. If I'd had the understanding I have now when I was going through my stressful period I would have dealt with it all in a very different way.

One of my reasons for writing this book is to pass on what I have learned so that hopefully others will benefit. But I must also keep in mind that, because of what happened to me in the past, I am now a different person.

My journey has been an extremely difficult one and one that I wouldn't change for anything. We are told that personal growth happens most profoundly through adversity and I would certainly agree 100% with that notion.

At no time was my journey constantly moving forward. There were times when I stood still and times when I took many steps backwards and had some really difficult episodes. But the saying two steps forward and one step back would adequately describe the general trend and so over time I made quite significant progress.

To help you to understand how I came to be so stressed that I needed 6 months to regain some of my equilibrium, I need to explain what I now see as my main stressor.

It is relatively easy to pinpoint the situations and events that cause us stress, but it is more difficult is to ascertain why. Not only why they caused us stress on a particular occasion but why we seemed unable to learn from our mistakes. It is easy to avoid mistakes in similar circumstances but not so easy when they seem to come in disguise.

Looking back it seems to me that I was actually sabotaging my own life. My high ethics were actually working against me. I never missed a trick and I couldn't let anything go. As a teacher this was particularly stressful as there were many occasions when it would have been beneficial to turn a blind eye to a child's behavior, especially if it wasn't having a lasting impact.

Similarly at home with my children, in my attempt to bring them up to be moral, upright human beings, my overly critical approach wasn't achieving my aims and objectives. Instead it was sabotaging my relationship with my kids.

Of course my own moral standpoint was – how could I possibly be in the wrong, after all I wanted my children to have a good upbringing and be good citizens. Nobody could argue with that. Again it was about being the best teacher, the best parent.

My husband has always been far more laid back than me and I would even get annoyed with him, feeling unsupported in my quest (as I saw it) to bring our children up well.

So what was going on here? Well I now realize that this was not about my children, the pupils at school, or my husband. It was all about me! It was my ego. It was my desire to look good, to be well respected in society. I am now aware that I had a massive lesson to learn. Of course at that time none of this was apparent to me and this way of behaving carried on for many years. Hence my chronic stress!

I have friends who would say I am being very hard on myself, but I see it as being honest. I have never expected more of myself than I was able to give at that time, but having realized what I was doing wrong meant that I needed to change and do things differently.

If I didn't take heed and change, my stress would continue. But if I was able to make some changes then my life would be less stressful and far healthier in the future. For me there really was no contest.

One of my "needs" in life has been to make a difference in other people's lives, hence the work I chose to do involved helping some of the most vulnerable young people in my city in an attempt to give them a better chance in life.

I also tended to be a person who found that little word "No" very difficult to say. Partly this was because I wanted to help but also if I said no I knew I would have to have a good reason to say no and that would mean making excuses, something I am not very convincing at. I now know that being assertive is a vital element of a life less stressed.

My lack of assertiveness in the past has disadvantaged me in many different ways. I hate conflict and so rather than challenge I would put up with certain behavior until my patience would be tried once too often and then I would "lose my rag". I would go from a very easy going person who likes to keep the peace to a totally irrational person who reacts often in a very hostile or sarcastic manner. Not a recipe for success in any walk of life.

Again I discovered that assertiveness was the only way forward if I was to change this unhelpful behavior.

29

I also became aware that although I am usually happy to do almost anything for anybody, if I am taken for granted I don't deal well with the situation and it is very easy for resentment to creep in.

I realized that the immortal words "to give and not to count the cost" were very pertinent to me and that was something I needed to take on board.

I mentioned earlier about having high expectations of myself. This in itself had an off-spin effect that I came to realize whilst working in the Pupil Referral Unit. Because I was prepared to work long hours, I unwittingly expected the same of my staff. Some, of course, did this anyway, but others were happy to just get by on the least amount of work as possible.

Needless to say this caused relationship problems which further exacerbated my stress.

So each of these aspects of my personality that had caused me to take the moral high ground were suddenly calling into question who I was. I became aware that they were actually working against me and were the major cause of my stress.

I remember around this time having my astrological chart done and one of the comments regarding what was happening to me at that time was that I was being forced to question values that I held dear. How true that was.

Of course writing all this down now in this way can so easily over simplify the situation. You might think – well if I had found out what was wrong all I had to do was change it. But these things don't happen overnight.

We often have to learn the same lesson over and over before we actually take notice.

It has taken me until today to feel that I truly understand what this all means and even then it is yet another lifetime's work making lasting changes.

TESTIMONIAL

"When my daughter did an assertiveness course I thought it was an odd idea, because she had never seemed to be lacking in confidence – but you never know what people are feeling inside. I read her course notes and realized that I have suffered from lack of assertiveness all my life. I think I would have suffered from less stress, less headaches, less self-doubt, and had a more enjoyable working life if I had realized earlier. I'm also – still – a perfectionist. I'm now determined that I will have an enjoyable retirement. I have accepted that nothing can really be perfect and I've lightened up on myself a lot. I do favors for friends and neighbors, but not at the expense of my own health, and I'm more able to say 'No' occasionally without feeling awful!"

Don, retired draughtsman

CHAPTER 7 - MY JOURNEY BACK TO HEALTH

HOW I ALLEVIATED MY STRESS

C3&O

At this point I would like to consider how I could have avoided my stress or dealt with it more effectively and then look at how I finally achieved a degree of homeostasis.

If I look back now to the time when I was in the midst of the stress I am frankly horrified that I didn't see the writing on the wall. Was it my stubborn pride, my inability to admit defeat, or maybe it was desire to continue to be the best I could be and allowing myself to be dominated by my own high expectations?

It was probably all of those things and a lot more besides.

I am certainly a different person now and would approach my situation quite differently.

HOW I LEARNED TO DEAL WITH MY STRESS MORE EFFECTIVELY

In order to deal with any stressful situation or any problem for that matter, the first step is to acknowledge that there is a problem in the first place. If you know anyone who has suffered from alcoholism, you will know that acknowledging that fact is the start of their path to healing. So for me, the moment I accepted that I was stressed and that it was affecting virtually every area of my life, was the moment my healing began.

- The single biggest problem that contributed to my stress was my personality, my desire to be the best I could be. On the face of it one might comment that being the best you can be is an admirable quality, but the problem arises when it gets out of hand. Accepting that I can't be as perfect as I would like to be has been a hard lesson for me, not only that but my idea of what being perfect meant wasn't necessarily everybody else's idea During my 6 months sick leave I booked myself onto a silent retreat for 5 days as part of my therapy. This proved to be a major influence in my ultimate healing as during that time of practicing just being with myself in the present moment, I started to realize that I didn't have to try so hard to be perfect. My friends and family would accept me for who I was whatever happened. I had to learn to trust and not want to always be in control. I still like to put in my best effort but I am now much kinder with myself if things don't work out as well as I would have liked and I am less concerned about what other people think about me. I am also more able to accept that sometimes a task is out of my reach. A little loving kindness for ourselves is an excellent antidote to stress.

- Being a full time head teacher and a mum to 3 teenagers is probably not exactly a recipe for success. Sometimes we put ourselves in impossible situations that have no hope of succeeding. Working part time would have been a solution and in the early days that was something I arranged by cutting my hours down to 4 days a week.

- Ofsted (government inspection) was certainly one of the straws that broke the camel's back. The stress that this caused was due in part to my previous lack of organization and time management. If I had been more organized and managed my time better I wouldn't have had such a massive task to deal with pre Ofsted. However, the off-spin of this was that because of Ofsted, my

34

paperwork was more organized and as such it had alleviated that area of stress in my future work.

- Dealing with pupils with emotional and behavioral problems brings with it problems that are hard to avoid. It was a steep learning curve every time we had a new intake, as each intake seemed to bring a different set of problems. So I am not sure what I could have done at the time to alleviate that stress, other than maybe find another job! One thing that did help was regularly re-evaluating our behavioral policy to deal with any new issues and being prepared to make regular changes if things weren't working. Being prepared to make changes of any sort is paramount to the success of any venture whether it is in business or health related.

- The effect of the menopause was something I was acutely aware of in one sense but I was totally unaware of how it was contributing to my stress. As somebody who won't take drugs, unless it is a lifesaving situation, meant that Hormone Replacement Therapy was out of the question. I decided to do some research into alternative remedies and discovered that certain herbs and homeopathic remedies were deemed to be helpful to regulate the hormones and I did in fact get some help from these methods.

Although, after my 6 months of "time out," I made some changes, as detailed above, that helped my situation, ultimately I was forced to make a big decision. After another two years of continued stress, particularly at work, re-organization within the Pupil Referral Service brought about a change that was completely unexpected. Based on my previous health record (due to the stress and the time out) the head of the Behavioral Service decided that for all concerned it would be better if I didn't continue in my present job. Initially I was offered the headship of a smaller Pupil Referral Unit, but subsequently I was given another option which was to accept a generous severance agreement, without prejudice.

Initially both options seemed unpalatable as I felt as though I had failed, and I felt aggrieved and angry with those who were asking me to make this decision. But somehow the option to accept a severance agreement seemed like an opportunity I couldn't afford to miss, so I decided to swallow my pride and accept.

Although it took me a long time to come to terms with my new found freedom, it was the best decision I ever made and I am convinced it saved my health and maybe even my life. I can only liken it to someone in a difficult stressful marriage who struggles with the ultimate decision to get divorced, feels bereaved for a time but eventually realizes that they now have the freedom to rebuild their lives. As often happens at these times it is not uncommon to eventually wonder what took you so long and why you didn't do it years ago!

After my premature retirement from my work, to help restore my life to some sort of normality, I used a range of different strategies. Initially it felt as though I had exchanged one set of stresses for another. A very busy stressful job is one thing but getting up every day with nowhere to go and nothing to do to occupy my time brought stresses of its own.

My children had by now left home to go to university and were leading their own lives elsewhere, my husband was still working, as were all my friends, and I was left "home alone". I felt a sense of bereavement for my job which had become who I was. I was the Head of the Pupil Referral Unit and that was largely my life. Now it had gone. I thought I would be relieved, but I wasn't. I was lost like a rudderless boat, with no plan and no purpose. I was completely taken by surprise at my reaction and to how stressful that could be.

I realized that up until that point I had had a title and function in life. I had been a daughter, a wife, a mother and a head-teacher. I had identified myself with those titles and now that the title head-teacher had gone, I was left naked and vulnerable.

I am sure I am not the only person who has retired or lost their job to feel that sense of loss. However, now it was time for me to find out who the real me was, a task I didn't relish at the time, but a task that has been one of the most interesting, illuminating and beneficial periods of my life.

Nine years have passed since that time, and many changes have taken place that have brought me to where I am today. None of it has been easy, but all of it has been very worthwhile.

❦

"It's not uncommon to wonder what took you so long and why you didn't do it years ago!"

❦

CHAPTER 8

THE LONG JOURNEY TO SPIRITUAL AND EMOTIONAL HEALTH AND PHYSICAL WELLBEING

CR&O

My journey to health and wellness is still far from over, but over the last 9 years I feel I have made a significant inroad into that journey. The journey has largely been a journey inward, a journey of self awareness and self discovery that has changed the way I look at the world and the way I respond.

If I looked back at the issues that were originally causing my stress, apart from my personality, all of the others had now disappeared from my life. I no longer had a stressful job, my children had left home and were no longer troublesome teenagers and in fact were very supportive of my current situation.

I had by now got though the worst of the menopause and although I was having to come to terms with the loss of my job and the practicalities of rebuilding my life, I knew that there had to be an internal change if I wanted to achieve the peace and inner contentment I so desired.

I don't remember having specific thoughts or a plan of action, but just an inner knowing that I was being called to re-evaluate my life, and, as often happens when we start to trust the process, opportunities appear before us and our next step becomes obvious.

I am a firm believer in the holistic approach to healing and the importance of healing the body, mind and spirit. The body is a more obvious one, but the mind has always seemed to me to be related to the emotions and the spiritual to the inner journey of awareness self discovery, and finding the true essence within.

I know some people like to think of religious practice as the spiritual journey and indeed this may help some people, but for me it is more than that, as will become evident as we discuss that section of my story

Because I feel that physical healing can only happen as a result of healing the mind and spirit as well as the body I am going to start with my emotional healing, followed by spiritual healing and culminating in the physical healing.

EMOTIONAL HEALING

I don't remember now how I came by a book called *The Journey* by Brandon Bays, but it was the start for me of what I can only describe as my emotional healing. I found out that she was coming to London for a weekend workshop and so I booked myself onto the workshop.

The Journey is a process that takes you on a staged journey within, helping to clear emotional issues that have held you back, preventing your full potential from flourishing.

During my first *Journey* process, I discovered my deepest emotion was anger. I was so very angry with everyone, my close family in particular who put such great store in my ability to cope and to be the strong one and solve everyone's problems, that I was actually sinking under the strain, trying to live up to their expectations of me.

What came first the chicken or the egg? Did I engender that expectation by setting myself up as some sort of paragon of virtue or did their expectations give me the message that I had to be strong for all of us? I guess I will never know, though I have a sneaky feeling it may well be the first of the two.

However, what I did realize was that my response to this situation was detrimental to all concerned and that it was actually ok to make some changes. I needed to be more vulnerable and not be afraid to make mistakes or say no.

A very heavy burden was lifted from me during that weekend and I went away with the knowledge that, given time, I would be able to make changes that would benefit us all.

Over the first few years of my retirement I did several *Journey* processes all of which were very revealing and very helpful. A bit like the layers of an onion, I kept peeling them back to find out what was there.

A lot of my emotional issues were around resentment and a lack of forgiveness, particularly regarding the staff who caused me so much anxiety and also those in higher management position who were responsible for what I saw as a lack of support, and the ultimate decision to re-organize the Service I worked for and orchestrate my removal from my job.

I came to understand that each had their own reason for their behavior and that I had been an integral part of the creation of the problem, something I hadn't been aware of at the time.

I was now able to forgive them and myself, and to move on with my life. To put things in perspective this part of the process probably took me about 5 years to achieve.

So you will see these things do not happen overnight. Sometimes you may not even be aware of the progress you are making until one day you are aware that those feelings/emotions are no longer there.

SPIRITUAL HEALING

I think spiritual healing or one's spiritual journey is probably the most misunderstood and the most difficult to understand of the three. My own spiritual journey started well before my episode of chronic stress. In fact I would say it probably began when I was a teenager, but I didn't recognize it as such at the time.

I have always had an interesting relationship with religion, ranging from absolute acceptance to complete rejection. I have always valued the Biblical stories and the teachings, but have tended to question the dogma and what I see as the man made aspects of religion. I believe, at times, that has obscured my spiritual growth and although I have now moved away from the church to find out what is right for me, there were many aspects of my experience within the church that were of great benefit to me over the earlier years.

I mentioned earlier that during my 6 months sick leave I had taken time to do a 5 day silent retreat. The retreat was in fact a religious retreat, called an Ignatian retreat, based on the spiritual exercises of Saint Ignatius Loyola. It is an approach to making decisions and a practical guide to everyday life and it is lead by an individual retreat director, on this occasion a nun.

During this time I was able to dig a little deeper into myself and start the process of truly understanding who I was and what my motivating factors were. In the daily silence it was amazing how much was revealed to me by simply listening, some would say to the voice of God, others would say to your inner voice, or the still small voice within. Others believe they are one and the same thing. I would tend to concur with that opinion.

There are many such tools available to help you on your spiritual journey, and it is important to understand that that is all they are, tools to help you. Some will speak to you and others will not. Most will help you so far and then you will need to find something else to take you to the next stage of understanding. But please remember that this is a life's journey and more importantly it is about the journey and not the destination.

You may at this point be wondering what this has to do with stress and stress relief. I mentioned earlier about how we sabotage ourselves with our learnt behavior or the personality we have developed to deal with the problems life throws at us. This is what causes most of our stress, the choices we make based on who we are and our past experience. Our spiritual journey is about understanding ourselves, getting to know who we really are as opposed to the ego personality we have developed, and making intelligent informed choices. Once we have mastered this, our lives will automatically be less stressful and may even become stress free depending on how far our journey takes us. In my opinion this is what life is all about. Even if you don't agree, please stay with me and I will try to explain further what I mean.

Just to recap, I explained earlier that I was sabotaging my own life because of my beliefs.

- I believed that I needed to be the best I could be in everything I did.
- I always thought I was right because I had given everything so much thought.
- I was silently disappointed with others when they didn't live up to my high expectations.
- More often than not I was non assertive because I didn't want to create conflict.
- I believed that to be a good person I had to keep the peace but often resented the outcome of "peace at any price".

43

It has taken me many years of being aware of what I was doing to finally realize and understand that it was actually my ego that was sabotaging me.

The ego is the personality we have developed throughout our lives. It is basically an illusion of who we really are and it is also the enemy of change. The ego avoids change because it believes so strongly in who it thinks we are, whereas our true self is happy for change. The true self lives in the present moment and isn't prone to thinking, or living in the past with all our past memories.

I read a quote recently that said:

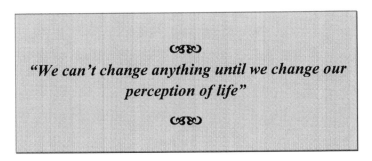

"We can't change anything until we change our perception of life"

I found that quote very profound and it made me realize that change starts from within, not from external circumstances. If we could stop thinking and start just enjoying the experience in the present moment we would start to move away from the ego and venture into the true essence of who we truly are.

When I was doing some research about the ego, one particular sentence stood out to me regarding my own situation.

> ⚭
>
> *"The self doesn't compare, whereas the ego thinks it is right and others are wrong."*
>
> ⚭

It was when I read that, that bells starting ringing for me. I suddenly realized that my ego thinking was preventing me from growing spiritually as a person, and was keeping me stuck in my habitual behavior. The ego is made up of our thoughts, the habits we form over the years and the opinions we gather as we experience life. We set a lot of store by all of that as we get older thinking that it is life's experience that makes us wiser than our younger counterparts, without realizing how it is making us rigid and set in our ways.

If we can start to live in the present moment and let go of the ego, we can enjoy just "being" without comparing or judging or having opinions or thinking we are right. We can let go of all the effort we put into life and enjoy being aware and open to life's experiences that are beyond thought.

When I realized what this actually meant I almost felt my stress melt away. However, understanding the words and being able to let go of the ego and live in the present moment are two ends of the spectrum. It requires daily practice and requires us to bring ourselves back to the present moment whenever we catch ourselves thinking, or getting into that "ego mode".

I am relatively new to this concept at the moment but it has served to explain a lot about my past behavior and I am very excited about the difference it could make to my life as I embark on this daily practice of mindful meditation.

Meditation has in fact been a very big part of my life over the last 10 years. For many years I was a member of the secular order of Carmelites. The Carmelite tradition is very much one of meditation and silence and I have attended monthly meditations and several Carmelite retreats throughout the year, as well as daily practice of 20 minutes silent meditation.

I was also lucky enough to have a friend, who sadly is no longer with us, who had a small meditation room in his home and I would regularly join him and his wife for meditation. We would, generally start with a walking meditation around the garden and then we would convene in the meditation room for a period of silence.

This period of my life was around the time of my retirement from my work and I am sure it had a major part to play in my recovery.

During this time I came across a retreat centre about an hour from my home town that specialized in Enneagram workshops and retreats. The Enneagram is a spiritual tool for understanding who you are and who you are meant to be.

It is based on a geometric diagram that is joined together in a dynamic way. The Enneagram helps you to identify your vice and helps you to find your virtue. It is by no means a definitive tool but it is a very positive way of helping you to lead a more contented life.

Over the last decade I have attended numerous workshops and retreats all of which have helped me on my inner journey of discovery. It is not easy to accept your vices but it is a very necessary process if you are to discover your essence, the shining diamond within. The workshops would always involve what was called "body work", each exercise aimed at developing awareness and helping each person to center and find their equilibrium.

I feel very privileged to have had access to so many wonderful processes, all of which have helped me to reach the level of health I have today

PHYSICAL HEALING

The problem with stress is it wrecks the adrenal glands, in some cases beyond the point of no return. In other words adrenal exhaustion sets in and it can take years before the damage can be repaired – if at all, especially if changes aren't made in the way you live your life. However all is not lost and with hard work and dedication it is possible to restore the body to an acceptable degree of homeostasis.

The body is an amazing machine and believe it or not it is actually programmed to heal itself. However this will only happen if the conditions for healing are implemented and then maintained, and that means looking at your lifestyle and making the necessary changes to allow the healing to take place.

Apart from the emotional and spiritual healing we have already discussed, changes that are physical in nature also need to take place. By this I am referring to diet and nutrition, exercise, supplements that may be necessary to help your body to redress the balance and also physical therapies that can aid the healing process.

Stress has a habit of using up all our reserves in more ways than one and it isn't unusual to find that there are major deficiencies in the chronically stressed individual.

Unfortunately most of us are looking for a quick fix for whatever ails us, and chronic stress is no exception. We tend to think that if we make a few changes then everything will be alright. That may be the case with acute stress but when the chronic condition reveals itself after years of stressful living, it can take a very long time to recover. Remember it has taken years to get to this stage and so inevitably it will be a long road back to full health.

NUTRITION

As I have a nutritional qualification (Dip ION) I had always thought that I had a healthy diet but further investigation proved that it wasn't as healthy as I had imagined. Most of my physical symptoms appeared to be stress related, frequent headaches, occasional but regular constipation (every few weeks), minor digestive problems, aching joints, and skin irritations.

However no matter how healthy I might have thought my diet was the symptoms persisted. I also suffered from bouts of lethargy and lack of motivation.

I tried many different ways of dealing with these symptoms until one day I decided to undergo some tests to find out what my nutritional and hormonal status was and whether I might have any allergies or intolerances I had previously been unaware of.

I wasn't surprised to discover that my cortisol levels were very low especially in the mornings, which explained why I found it so difficult to get going at the start of the day. I was also not surprised to find I had mild and medium intolerances to certain foods. What did surprise me was that I tested positive for gluten intolerance.

Now I felt I had something tangible to work with and could make some sensible informed changes to my diet. I immediately took gluten out of my diet (wheat, oats, barley, rye) and replaced it with other products such as rice, buckwheat (not a wheat despite its name) millet and quinoa.

The intolerances, and in particular the wheat, had been adding an extra burden/stress on my already stressed body, so removing them made a big difference. I no longer have aching joints and my digestive system has been far more efficient. I would even go so far as to say I have had more energy and less brain fog.

Of course when we take one thing out of our diets the chances are we are likely to replace it with something equally bad for us. So this is something you need to be aware of. I have noticed a lot of gluten free advice and gluten free recipes tend to be replacements for cakes, biscuits, pastries etc.

Although you are avoiding the gluten you are probably doing as much harm by introducing sugary foods and foods high in simple carbohydrates that cause hypoglycemia (low blood sugar) Inevitably this can be devastating for you health if you are working to improve your adrenal fatigue.

I also discovered that I was very low in beneficial bacteria in my gut. I had the presence of yeasts which needed to be balanced with probiotics, so I started to make my own yoghurt and sauerkraut, and for a while I took probiotic supplements to boost my good bacteria and ultimately my immune system.

In addition to the probiotic, I took a B Complex vitamin, commonly known as the stress vitamin. B vitamins are depleted during stressful episodes and they are needed for the body to make energy. I also took vitamin D3 to boost my immune system.

There are many other supplements that nutritionists advise for stress related problems but these were the ones that I instinctively felt I needed. In all cases if you are going to go down this route then I would advise you seek the advice of a qualified nutritional practitioner who can ascertain your personal needs. Even though I am a qualified practitioner myself I still sought the advice of a practitioner who was able to help me to see things more objectively.

You may be wondering exactly how this is relevant to your stressed state, but it is my belief that my stress was in part responsible for my poor nutritional status. Nothing ever happens in isolation. Most problems are multifaceted and stress is no exception. By redressing the balance I hoped to improve my overall health.

So many stress books teach you external strategies to deal with your stress, such as to relax, eat well, find a hobby, do some exercise etc etc, but very few teach you how to look beneath the surface and deal with the problem from the inside out.

While the more basic strategies can be beneficial for counteracting stress as it occurs, they are probably more effective for acute rather than chronic stress. For a lasting solution you have to change your perception of your life and combine your inner knowing with the choices you are making.

As soon as you can feel like a peaceful, contented person on the inside you will start to make the right decisions about other choices in your life such as the food you eat. A healthy mind will choose healthy, life giving foods – it is as simple as that.

CЗ80

A lot of gluten free advice and gluten free recipes tend to be replacements for cakes, biscuits, pastries, etc.

You are probably doing as much harm by introducing sugary foods and foods high in simple carbohydrates that cause hypoglycemia (low blood sugar).

This can be devastating for you health if you are working to improve your adrenal fatigue.

CЗ80

EXERCISE

There is no disputing that exercise has the ability to engender that feel good factor. It releases endorphins, otherwise known as the brains feel good neurotransmitters. Exercise is undoubtedly good for our overall health and as far as stress is concerned it doesn't matter if that exercise is walking, swimming, yoga or playing a game of tennis, it is an invaluable part of your stress relief program.

For my own part I was lucky enough to be a member of a leisure complex and found swimming to be an excellent de stressor. I found it was almost like a meditative practice as I was able to concentrate on my stroke and my breathing and the rest of life just passed me by.

I am also lucky in that I love playing tennis and found this to be a great way to take my mind off what was going on in the rest of my life.

In addition I walk regularly and have from time to time engaged in the practice of yoga. I know from my own experience that yoga is an excellent exercise for stress relief as it works all areas of the body and has a deep meditative element. Although I have enjoyed the practice it is not a discipline that I am easily drawn to.

PHYSICAL THERAPIES

During my healing process I have experienced various different physical therapies, all of which have helped although, as always, some have helped more than others.

Massage – In the early days I found massage would ease the tension in my body and left me feeling far more relaxed. Aromatherapy massage is particularly beneficial as the masseuse uses aromatherapy oils to suit the needs of the individual person.

Shiatsu – Is a similar type of therapy to acupuncture and as such has been an integral part of traditional Chinese medicine for many years. As with most holistic therapies the aim of Shiatsu is to support and strengthen the natural healing ability of the body. It is a therapy that aims to balance psychological, emotional and spiritual well being. I found Shiatsu to be an extremely relaxing therapy and one that I am sure was an integral part of my healing.

Indian Head Massage - Because headaches were a big part of my stress picture, I found Indian Head Massage to be extremely beneficial in alleviating the tension causing my headaches.

Colonic Irrigation- I am well aware that this is a therapy that many people would shy away from, but I have found it to be a particularly cleansing therapy in more ways than one. Because I had been so stressed, my body had ceased to function efficiently and I constantly felt toxic. Colonic irrigation cleansed me of that toxic feeling and also had quite a profound effect on my ability to think more clearly and move forward in my life. My therapist who was also a **kinesiologist** was able, through sensitive muscle testing, to ascertain which foods I needed to avoid and also which supplements would be most beneficial for me to take.

I still have a very long way to go in my healing process, but interestingly I think I have made some very big strides during the process of researching and writing this book. Somehow relating my story in this way has helped me to better understand what has happened and given me a clearer way forward. I hope it has also helped you in some small way.

I would like to finish by quoting a piece of prose (next page) written in 1927 by Max Ehrmann. It is a wonderful spiritual text that has become a mantra for my new way of living. It speaks plainly of how we should conduct our lives if we truly want a life that is less stressed.

DESIDERATA

ೞ

Go placidly amid the noise and haste, and remember what peace there may be in
silence.
As far as possible, without surrender, be on good terms with all persons.
Speak your truth quietly and clearly; and listen to others, even the dull and ignorant;
they too have their story.

Avoid loud and aggressive persons; they are vexations to the spirit.
If you compare yourself with others, you may become vain and bitter;
for always there will be greater and lesser persons than yourself.

Enjoy your achievements as well as your plans.
Keep interested in your career, however humble; it is a real possession in the changing
fortunes of time.

Exercise caution in your business affairs, for the world is full of trickery.
But let this not blind you to what virtue there is; many persons strive for high ideals;
and everywhere life is full of heroism.

Be yourself. Especially, do not feign affection.
Neither be critical about love; for in the face of all aridity and disenchantment it is as
perennial as the grass.
Take kindly the counsel of the years, gracefully surrendering the things of youth.

Nurture strength of spirit to shield you in sudden misfortune.
But do not distress yourself with imaginings.
Many fears are born of fatigue and loneliness.
Beyond a wholesome discipline, be gentle with yourself.

You are a child of the universe, no less than the trees and the stars;
you have a right to be here.
And whether or not it is clear to you, no doubt the universe is unfolding as it should.

Therefore be at peace with God, whatever you conceive Him to be,
and whatever your labors and aspirations, in the noisy confusion of life keep peace
with your soul.
With all its sham, drudgery and broken dreams, it is still a beautiful world.

Be careful. Strive to be happy.
© Max Ehrmann 1927 – cc

MEDICAL DISCLAIMER

ABOUT THE AUTHOR

ೞ

Janet Matthews is a retired head-teacher of a school for pupils with emotional and behavioral problems. She has a diploma (Dip ION) in nutritional practice from the Institute of Optimum Nutrition in London and has had an active interest in health and personal development for many years.

Her other qualifications include:-

- Life Coaching Certificate
- Life Coaching Diploma
- Enneagram Teacher (part 1)
- MBTI Practitioner
- Metabolic Typing Practitioner

Janet has been writing online as a ghostwriter since 2007. She has several health related blogs of her own and has been a guest writer for other blogs and websites on the subject of health and well- being.

Is Stress YOUR Silent Killer? is her first book.

Her second book *Really Healthy Gluten Free Living*, which is now available on Amazon, explores how healthy gluten free diets really are and offers a protocol for healing the gut and outlines a healthier approach to a gluten free life. It also includes **32 healthy gluten free recipes**.

Janet has plans for many more in a series of self help health and wellbeing books. You can find information on her up-and-coming publications on her website: **http://your-healthy-options.com.**

RESOURCES FOR FURTHER READING

☙❧

BOOKS

The Power of Now – Eckhart Tolle
A New Earth – Eckhart Tolle
Personality Types – Riso and Hudson
The Enneagram –Understanding Yourself and Others in Your Life –
Helen Palmer
The Journey – Brandon Bays

JANET'S WEBSITES

http://your-healthy-options.com

http://isstressyoursilentkiller.blogspot.co.uk

http://meditation-practices.com

Janet would love to hear your thoughts. Feel free to email her at:

janet@your-healthy-options.com

INDEX

☙❧

28732818R00040

Made in the USA
Lexington, KY
30 December 2013